the color love journal

a gift for your health and happiness

by thea keats beaulieu

G C Communication

9/95

Published by G C Communication
New York, NY 10013.

This book was made possible by a Grant from
Synaesthetics LTD
a Non-Profit Art Foundation.

Text, Drawing and Cover Design by David Postelnik.

Library of Congress Cataloging-in-Publication Data

Beaulieu, Keats Thea
The Color Love Journal

ISBN 0-9632758-0-1

Bookstore

About the Author

Thea Keats Beaulieu is an active dancer, movement therapist, teacher, and Polarity practitioner. She performs as principle dancer with the Isadora Duncan Dance Company of New York and San Francisco. Her dance integrates the natural rhythms and expressions of Nature and the Elements. She holds degrees in English and Dance from the University of Wisconsin. Her unique contribution in the Healing Arts is expressing Dance and Color through the Five Elements.

Thea Keats Beaulieu currently lives and practices in New York City with husband, John, and puppy, Hubie, and teaches workshops internationally.

Contents

As a psychiatrist, practising wholistically I often use color with my patients.

The Color Love Journal is the best guide of its kind on the journey of Self Healing. It provides sheer joy in reading as well as valuable tools to bring more peace, love, acceptance and self improvement to your daily life.

It will delight you and your inner child.

Elisabeth Louisa Macrae, M.D., New York

• • • • • • • • • • • •

The Color Love Journal provides a wonderful opportunity to bring a new dimension to your life through developing an energetic relationship with color.

The Journal is easy to read and the results are like a rainbow shower. We are surrounded by colors.

Thea shows us how to tune into life's color palette. She then invites us into the artistry of life and encourages us to create our own unique colorful reality.

John Beaulieu, N.D., R.P.P.
Author of "Music and Sound in the Healing Arts"

Preface

I would like to thank the many colorful people in my life who have helped to create the Color Love Journal.

Many thanks to:

• my husband and teacher *John Beaulieu,* for his love, support, encouragement and dedication to the artistic nature of all things and how it can serve others.

• *to Lynn Ritchie and Don Billett,* who spent many hours reading and editing and supporting the making of the book from its inspiration to making it real.

• *to Caton Whipple,* for his wonderful and magical Color Guide.

• *to Dr. Randolph Stone,* founder of Polarity Therapy and *Isadora Duncan,* the founder of Modern Dance.

• to my *puppy Hubie* who did not, in fact, chew up any part of this book in any of its stages.

• to all my dancing friends and teachers - *Adrienne, Mignon, Hortence, and Julia.*

• *to all my clients,* who taught me to trust by their own experiences.

• *to all the guiding magical spirits* who gave me inspiration in countless untold ways.

• *to my mother* the painter, who taught me at a young age to appreciate the colors she created all around her.

• *to my father,* who taught me how to explain the language of inspiration and make the magic real.

• *to Lars,* whose photographic eye lent a keen view.

• *to Lin Haley,* my magical friend from the Vermont Hills, for her wonderful artistic eye and truly inspiring friendship.

• to all my wonderful friends in Switzerland, *Andreas and Brigitta, Yargos, Michelle, Heidy, Sandy, Butz, Catherine, and Monique.*

• *to Laura Day, Leor, Roz, Joya, Elsa, Lee and Judy, and Dr. Elisabeth Macrae.*

• *to Terry Hayes for copyediting services*

• *and to all my dear friends and family* who have lent their magic, inspiration and insights so that this gift of a book could come into being.
Thea Keats Beaulieu

Introduction

Through the ages we have been blessed with color. Colors make us happy. Have you ever noticed how putting on brightly colored clothing can cheer you up? Imagine the expression on a child's face when he or she is handed a rainbow lollipop or a bunch of brilliantly colored balloons. **Color Love** presents a new concept of choosing and wearing Colors to directly affect your physical and emotional well-being.

Now I'd like you to imagine for a moment that you are sitting on a beautiful beach under a palm tree and you are looking out at the water. It is a hot summer's day and as you watch the turquoise blue water lap up gently on the white sand and feel the warm sun against your skin, suddenly, you see the dark clouds roll over the water. It starts to rain, a sun shower, and as you cover yourself with your towel, you look up and see, in the blink of an eye, a miraculous arching of colors glinting in the sunlight across the water, red, blue, yellow, green, violet, a perfect blending, a rainbow of colored light arching from heaven to earth and water. How does it make you feel?

Color. The Magic of Colors. The Love of Colors. Color Love.

This is a book of stories, stories of colors and love and the elements that surround us and are within us.

The purpose of this book on colors is to present a guide for you, to enable you to become more conscious about choosing colors that will directly affect your physical as well as emotional well-being. I want you to have as many tools as you can to make yourself look and feel your very best. This book begins a process of inquiry and exploration that hopefully will continue for the rest of your lives. How you can make yourself feel more, enjoy more, and have more, of the things you desire to have in life. We will explore how many different ways you can enrich the life you have been given, and how to deeply appreciate yourself as well as the people around you.

It is my intention that through the miraculous study of color, you will find love, and it is my desire to be of service to you, to guide you so that you will become happier, more successful and more fulfilled, with every area of your life sparkling with Color... And Love.

Thea

The Color Love Journal

The **Color Love Journal** provides a way for you to blend the miraculous world of color energy into your daily life. Contained in this workbook are deep relaxation exercises, color visualizations, and positive affirmations. Through the use of these powerful aids you will learn how to use new mind-body techniques to help enrich and expand your awareness of your daily life.

Each color in the world vibrates at its own energy level and influences our state of being.

The **Color Love Journal** is based on these energies and how they relate to nature's elements: *Ether, Air, Fire, Water, and Earth.*

By deepening your awareness of Color and the Elements, you can balance your inner self with the outer world around you. Space is provided in the Journal so that you can actively participate, become explorers, space travelers in the unknown, to discover new and exciting things about yourself.

So let us begin to enjoy our Color journey!

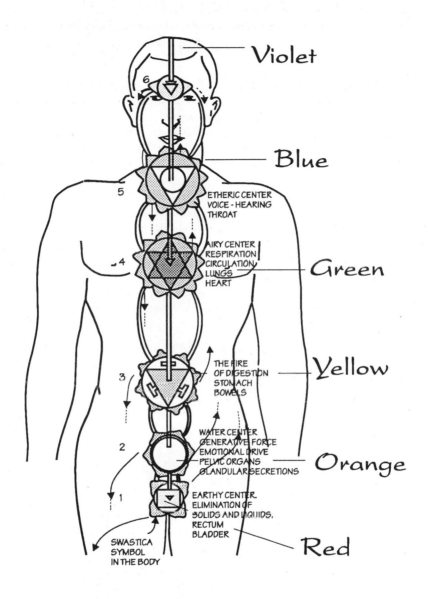

Violet

Blue

6

5

ETHERIC CENTER
VOICE - HEARING
THROAT

AIRY CENTER
RESPIRATION
CIRCULATION
LUNGS
HEART

Green

4

3

THE FIRE
OF DIGESTION
STOMACH
BOWELS

Yellow

2

WATER CENTER
GENERATIVE FORCE
EMOTIONAL DRIVE
PELVIC ORGANS
GLANDULAR SECRETIONS

Orange

1

EARTHY CENTER.
ELIMINATION OF
SOLIDS AND LIQUIDS,
RECTUM
BLADDER

Red

SWASTICA
SYMBOL
IN THE BODY

**This chart shows how our bodies relate
to the elements.**

Color as a Healing Vibration

The Vibratory Qualities of Color

Colors are vibrations, like thoughts and sound. Each color has its own pulse, a vibratory quality that affects our physical, mental and sensory mind-bodies. Just as a sound can vibrate sand on a plate into a beautiful pattern *(John Beaulieu. "Music and Sound in the Healing Arts". Station Hill Press.)* color also has the same ability to vibrate and penetrate deep into our cellular structures.

There have been numerous researchers exploring this vibratory nature of color and its effects on healing. Roland Hunt, a noted researcher, author of the *"Seven Keys to Color Healing" (Harper and Row.)* says: "There are seven spectrum colors and seven major glandular or energy centers in the body. These centers are called *chakras*. Each chakra controls a specific area of physical or mental health - each has its own spectrum color vibration. When the correct color is applied to the corresponding chakra center - the body and soul respond by repairing or revitalizing the area in need."

Edwin Babbit (born in 1838), a noted author and researcher of Color, wrote volumes of books and research and case studies on the *"The Principles of Light and Color". University Books.*

In ancient Egypt color played an integral part in the healing practices as well as their spiritual development. In the Healing Temples of Light and Color in Egypt, colors were prescribed as remedies for many ailments. There is also evidence of the use of color for healing in the ancient civilizations of Greece, India and China.

For centuries people have been exploring the amazing effect of color, its healing properties and its abilities to affect our moods, health, spiritual, and mental well-being.

It has been observed that many blind people can feel colors. This is due again to their vibratory quality. It is also this vibratory quality that enables deaf people to feel or hear music. This pulse of color has the power similar to a sound wave to reorganize, re-connect, and change the way we perceive, act and behave in our daily life. Just as sand vibrates into a beautiful pattern when it is vibrated under a plate, so color too has the potential to create new patterns within us. If how we think creates our reality, if our thoughts do effect our environment, if what we say affects the people around us, then take this journey with colors, letting them guide you, and experience their miraculous power and influence.

The Story of Color and the Elements

Sit back in your comfortable chair and allow all the thoughts of the day to drift by. Now let us enter another reality — a reality of colors and the elements. Let's go back to the beginning, even before life as we know it, where there were only the elements: *Ether, Air, Fire, Water and Earth.* Each element corresponds with a color and also has a psychological quality.*

The elements surround us and are within us. For example, **Ether is Blue,** it is space, the infinite space that supports all the other elements, the deep silence in the forest,the calming peace that comes with deep relaxation.

Air is green, fast-moving like the wind, it represents our mind, our hearts and our intellects.

Fire is Yellow. It warms us and like a tiger leaping, it is our ability to take action, to be enthusiastic and determined about what we do.

Water is Orange and flows all around us, winding over the rocks, creating new paths and possibilities through the land. It flows on and on like a dolphin swimming. It governs our sexuality, our creative abilities, and gives us nourishment.

Earth is Red. It supports us, gives us a foundation, makes us feel secure. Like cows grazing in a field, it is slow moving. It is the quality of Earth that allows us to create structure, limitations and boundaries in our lives.

All the elements are around us, as well as within us. It is through the concept of the elements that we seek balance within ourselves and our environment. We must irrigate a desert in order to grow food. So we can apply the same principal to ourselves.

If we have too much water (orange) in our bodies, we may become blubbery and fat. We must learn to have more of the earth vibration (red), for earth is the element that gives us the ability to set limits on what we eat, and therefore enables us to maintain the weight we desire.

Theory of the Elements based on principles of Polarity Therapy Dr. Randolph Stone "Health Building". CRCS Publication, Sebastopos, CA

Naturally, the environment seeks balance. With our ever increasing technological society we must put more of our attention on maintaining balance.

We must learn to accept and allow expression for each of the elements that flow through us. The elements can be merciless, as we have seen in our hurricanes and earthquakes. If we interfere or suppress them, they may express themselves in ways we may not like. If we suppress our fire, our expression of anger and our ability to act and assert ourselves, through the use of alcohol or drugs, it will seek balance on its own, and it could, over the years, develop into physical symptoms or illness. (Suppressed fire could show up as an ulcer or arthritis or any inflammation in the body).

It is toward this concept that this book attempts to explain the qualities of the elements with their colors and meanings so that you will have another way to allow the expression of each element so that you can become as comfortable with fire **(yellow)** *(anger, assertion)* as you are with water **(orange)** *(emotions, feelings)*.

This book does not attempt to diagnose, prescribe, or treat illness. It will teach you a new way of looking and feeling about yourself, so that you can learn a new flexibility, another way to maintain your well-being.

I would like to add the colors *white, black, pink and violet* into our color palate. **White** is the color that adds lightness, purity, and cleanliness to form. If you wear all white you draw attention to yourself. Any color that goes towards white adds this quality. **Black** is mysterious, seductive and protective. Any color that goes towards black, or is darker, adds more of this quality. **Pink** is red and white together. **Violet** symbolizes wisdom, inner strength, and guidance.

(See color chart on back cover for more about these colors).

The Color Love Process

The Five Steps:

1. Breath

2. Visualization

3. Conscious Daily Exercises

4. Affirmation

5. Appreciation

The **Color Love Process** is the synthesis of many years of study. I have found basic principles behind effective systems of creating positive results in human behavior.

Drawing from many therapeutic, mind-body techniques, as well as principals from the ancient Greeks, I have combined and simplified my learnings into what I think works best on your Journey of Colors.

With practice, concentration and a willingness to trust and be open, I have found that with the **Color Love Process** miracles are indeed possible!

1. How to Use the Breath for Deep Relaxation

B reath is the key to life. It enables us to get in touch with our inner selves. When we become aware of our breathing, we can enter into a state of relaxation necessary for maintaining health. This state of relaxation leads us into a place of receptivity and openness which is the first step in our process.

To become aware of your breathing, sit in a comfortable position and put your focus on your breathing. Let your hands gently rest on your chest and abdomen and feel the breath rise and fall. Notice where you are breathing from. Now let your breath come in deeply letting the belly rise and fall. This is called *diaphramatic breathing.*

Now, at the same time imagine a cool air coming into your nostrils as you inhale and a warm air coming through your nose as you exhale, letting your breath fill your whole body, feeling your chest as well as abdomen rise and fall. This can be practiced a few minutes each day, especially in times of stress. Breathing for relaxation can be a great aid in balancing ourselves and staying centered.

In *Color Breathing* you must first find the color you need and want. You breathe in the color and feel it spread through your entire body. You can imagine that as you inhale the color it is in the center of your solar plexus and radiates out like rays of the sun, filling each and every one of your cells.

2. Visualizations are Powerful Tools That We Can Use to Make Positive Changes in Our Lives.

Visualizations are powerful tools we have in order to make needed and desired changes in our lives. When we visualize something, we create a mental picture for ourselves in a relaxed way, we picture those things in our creative imagination that we would like to change.

For example, if you are very tense, you may want to visualize yourself on a raft floating gently down the river, allowing your body to feel that wonderful sense of deep relaxation that comes when you are drifting on the water without the pressure of time.

To increase your ability to use the powerful tool of visualization let's do the following exercise. Imagine yourself in a situation where you were extremely happy, where you felt a wonderful aliveness, a wholeness, a joyousness, where you felt you were in perfect harmony, at one with yourself and the universe. Pick one situation and recall all the sounds; for example, birds singing, or the sound of the ocean. See all the people around you, all the objects, the environment you are in, see it all, and now feel all the physical sensations in your body while you are there enjoying that wonderful feeling of aliveness and wholeness and harmony.

Now color the whole situation. Take whatever color comes. Give a title to your experience, a title with a color and your name (Jane's Blue Happiness at the Sea.)

Practice this visualization to increase your ability to visualize.

In our Journal, there is a visualization for each color.

Be sensitive to your own spontaneous awareness of color that may be individual to you, be open to your own intuitive ability to visualize colors you may need to heal you or your situation at any given moment.

3. Affirmations

An affirmation is a positive statement that we say about ourselves in order to re-program our beliefs and thoughts. It is the power to visualize ourselves having the desired result we want in our life. We affirm that our life is already better and different.

I ask you at this point to be open and willing to assume that what we think can effect what we experience. For example, if we think we don't deserve love, then we continually have the experience of not feeling loved by others. An affirmation is a statement aimed at changing our thoughts, our basic beliefs so that we can create the positive changes we want in our lifes. If we want more love in our life, we may need to change our belief from, "I don't deserve love to - I feel loved".

To be effective, an affirmation can be written ten times in the morning when first awakening and/or right before going to sleep. You can say it aloud to yourself in front of mirror, or listen to it over and over on a tape you can make yourself. Repetition is the key. The more you repeat the affirmation the better.

The more you can visualize your desired state of being and allow yourself to trust and have faith that it can happen, in fact is happening now, the quicker the results will manifest in your life.

4. Conscious Daily Exercises

Each Color has an exercise for you to do daily to enhance the effects of Color in your daily life.

5. The Many Splendors of Giving Thanks - Appreciation

An integral part of our process and of the process of creating a healthy mind-body is to give thanks for what we already have and to trust in our own inner wisdom, that we know what is best for us.

It is important at this stage to see the changes you want. See them as already happening and feel your appreciation for this wonderful gift.

Lets Get Started

Let's say you wake up and you just can't get motivated. You feel lazy and you have a big presentation to make at work. You look on your chart and see the desired state of being enthusiastic, taking action. That fits. *The element is fire. The color is yellow.* Open to the section of your Journal for Yellow.

You are seeking balance by learning about this color. Use your workbook - honestly answer each question with the first things that come to mind. Writing things down helps to focus your mind. Than let go and relax. This is your time to let go, immerse yourself in the joy of colors, bathe your senses in your visualizations, slow down, smile and enjoy your Color Journey.

Color is personal. Use colors as a way to further strengthen your positive experiences, and to create a new and colorful you!

I want to thank you now for being open to this unique and special way of experiencing color.

I invite you all to experiment, experience, make changes and have fun!

Blue

Ether. . .
Self Expression. . .
Communication. . .
Opening up. . .
Deeply Understood
and Appreciated. .

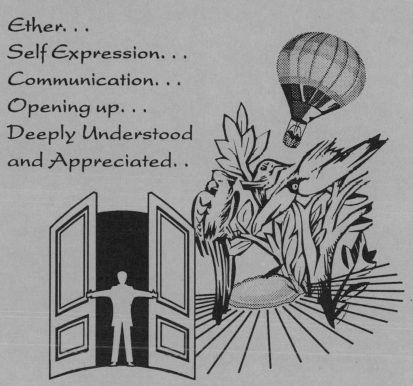

Blue is the Wonderful Color
of Deep Relaxation and Rest

The Element of Ether symbolizes our ability to express ourselves, how we communicate with other people. It is the feeling of expansion, of opening up, feeling free and unrestricted. It is the color of serenity. Blue has a calm, tranquil and soothing effect on the nervous system.

The Ether element opens up the space for the other elements to flow. Therefore blue gives the feeling of space, of lots of room to move in; it helps us to expand our awareness. When we feel stuck, blue can guide us to new possibilities in deeply relaxed and peaceful ways. . .

Color Visualization

N ow we are entering a time of Blue. I want you to sit down and relax now, each muscle in your body finding its own comfortable place. Imagine the color blue coming into your body, as a blue breath fills your lungs and your stomach and your rib cage expands, let blue flow through every organ of your body.

And as you breathe out, imagine that there is a silver pitcher suspended above your head and it is filled with a beautiful blue water, as blue as the most beautiful water you have ever seen on a warm summer's day, a turquoise, almost luminescent blue, and feel the warm blue water spilling down from the top of your head, through every part of your body as you relax even more deeply and let your mind go of all the thoughts of the day, everything dissolving into blue, as your body begins to relax even more deeply, you find yourself at the water's edge looking out at the vast blue sea, a turquoise, or blue as far as you can see. Sit back now and feel the expansiveness of infinite space. . .

As you listen to the deep silence, feel the space opening up in your body; even your joints are breathing, allowing movement to spring from your body quite naturally. Let all your organs bathe in this glorious blue liquid, and feel the space in your body opening up as you breathe in and breathe out.

See yourself wearing blue, a blue that you love. As you look out at the endless sea stretching toward the setting sun, you see a beautiful bluebird flying over the water, singing so sweetly; and he comes to rest gently on your shoulder. He speaks to you, telling you to let all those things inside you that need to come out, come out now, freely; all the things you meant to say, all the feelings you were afraid to feel, let them come now freely, safely, in their own appropriate time. You are so happy and you thank the little bluebird, and with a sigh you turn and face the sun, and let the sounds spill out across the water. . .

Conscious Daily Exercise

For Stress.

To gain Inner Strength, Inner Peace.

Become aware of your breathing.

Take another breath in and imagine a deep
blue sea surrounding you, let the blueness of the
water emanate from you like a ray of blue light,
swirling up from your feet, up your body all the
way to the top of your head and then let it spin
off into the sun. . .

Affirmation

- I express myself clearly.

- I am deeply understood and appreciated.

- I have plenty of space.

- I am enjoying the wonderful feeling of deep relaxation, knowing that everything is being taken care of.

- I enjoy the feeling of letting go.

- I trust myself.

- I am at peace.

Body Parts - Throat, Joints.
(Body Parts associated with each color based on work of Dr. Randolph Stone and Polarity Therapy.)

Appreciation

*Feel and see
yourself having the
effects you desire.*

Give Thanks.

Now write down all those people in your life that you feel you need to express yourself to. . .

And any situations now or in the past when you have felt trapped, smothered, unable to speak freely, closed in, or oppressed.

Are you tense, under stress, under what conditions?

With whom?

Give yourself all the space you need.

How do you breathe? (From your chest or your diaphram?)

Workbook

Personal Reflections.

Green

Love...
Healing...
Compassion...
Harmony...
Success...
Abundance...
Prosperity...

Green is the Color of the Air Element

Quick moving and fast, it stands for the intellect, the ability to see things clearly, discriminate and make choices.

Green also symbolizes prosperity, abundance, success. It is the heart, the ability to love, be compassionate, our ability to hear and be harmonious within ourselves.

It is the ability to make quick decisions, to move from one situation to another in your life with ease.

Green is like the movement of a butterfly or a bird, ever flying to new heights to gain a new perspective.

Color Visualization

Gazing into the Emerald Pool of love.

N ow find yourself a comfortable place to relax in. Let your body sink into a soft chair and allow your mind to drift as you take a deep breath in letting go of all the problems of the day as you breathe out. Let your facial muscles begin to relax, yes, that's it, let your jaw release. Go inside now and let your entire body relax, feel your feet on the ground and your back against the chair, feel the air against your skin and hear all the sounds around you right now. Let them be a part of your journey, as you breathe in and breathe out and allow yourself to go even deeper into this wonderful state of deep and peaceful relaxation. . .

Now see yourself standing in the middle of a great field filled with tall green grass as far as you can see, and see wind rippling through the grass making wave-like patterns, green waves all around you; feel the warm sun on your face as you gaze into a beautiful emerald pool as you breathe in the sweet smell of summer the green lushness so fresh after the rain has fallen. . . you see your own reflection shining with so much love in your eyes. . . and as you look up you see a white bird soaring across the blue sky, you watch as it lands way up on the tallest branches; a few leaves fall and you begin to run, feeling as light and buoyant as the bird, moving quickly through the green grass to catch a fallen leaf. . .

And now for a moment let those people and those situations in your life that need to be healed come into your thoughts. Take the time to really see yourself and those people clearly. See the love and compassion in your eyes. Now look in their eyes. Find the love. Now color the whole scene green in your imagination. Allow the color green to soak into your body and soothe you. Let it heal all the sore points in yourself and in your relationships. Breathe green into those parts. . .

Thank you. . .

We appreciate your willingness to explore, to journey to unknown parts of yourself, to be open to change and discover new things about yourself. . .

Conscious Daily Exercise

Do your breathing for relaxation as shown in the **Color Love Process** to get into a receptive state.

Picture the situation. The way it is now. Maybe you'd like more money, greater success, more appreciation; perhaps you'd really like to begin a new business venture. Be honest.

Now imagine the Color Green. Let it fill every part of your body. Imagine a green light surrounding you. Imagine your situation around prosperity, surround it with green.

Imagine the people, situations, including yourself in the process, that you would like to feel more love towards, compassion, or harmony with; surround them in green. Make sure you do this with your breathing.

Surround anyone who needs healing, including yourself, with the Color Green.

Affirm your new situation, as if it has already taken place. Choose the affirmation that fits best for you or make up one that is even more specific and write in the space provided in the notebook.

Give thanks. . . find the way that's most appropriate for you.

Affirmation

Choose the one most appropriate for you right now.

- **I am filled with love.**

- **I heal myself and others.**

- **I am compassionate.**

- **I am enjoying greater levels of abundance and prosperity in my life.**

- **Whatever I need comes to me in a safe and effortless way.**

Body Part - Heart, Lungs, Calves, Ankles

Appreciation

*See yourself
exactly the way
you'd like to be.*

Give thanks.

Workbook

In the following space make a list of those people in your life that you love.

Now list those people who you find most difficult to love and those situations in which you feel the least compassionate.

List any people, including yourself, who need healing at this time.

Workbook

Review your financial situation and write down any feelings, words, that would describe it right now... Would you like to be more prosperous? If so, write now exactly how you would like your life to be. Be as specific as you can.

Affirmations.

Choose the affirmation that attracts you the most or feel free to create a new one for yourself.

Workbook

Personal Reflections.

Yellow

Fire. . .
Action. . .
Purpose. . .
Enthusiasm. . .

Yellow is the Color of Fire

It is the ability to see things clearly.

It is the ability to take clear action with purpose, enthusiasm and optimism.

It is our movement out into the world.

It is our ability to stop thinking and go forward, the color of vision and the future. Yellow is the color of spontaneity, focused energy and fiery passion.

Color Visualization

The Leaping Tiger and the Buttercup

Now find a nice quiet place to sit back and relax, away from all the worries and cares of the day. Just let yourself lean back now, let the muscles in your jaw release, let your neck relax, let the tension around your eyes dissolve, melting into yellow daffodils waving in the breeze on a hot summers day.

As you gently and easily breathe in and breathe out, allow yourself to go to a place inside of yourself where there is only yellow, and as you breathe in the color yellow, imagine that you have just stepped into the most wondrous palace, a white castle rising up to the heavens. This wondrous castle is surrounded by millions of beautiful yellow flowers, their colors are so bright, daffodils, tulips, fields of yellow buttercups. . . and wildflowers everywhere.

You can't believe your eyes as you feel the hot sun on your face, a big ball of fire in the sky warms your fingers and toes, warms your tummy. . . and you hear the beautiful singing of a canary, so sweet, as it sits perched on the tip of a yellow daffodil and you feel the tips of its wing as you bend down to pick up a small delicate buttercup and you hold it under your chin.

As a child, as an adult, like the buttercup, you too can tell the truth and take action. And off in the distance a yellow tiger sits in the shadows; it spots its prey and with single-minded purpose it leaps. . .

Conscious Daily Exercise

Tune into your breathing.

Surround yourself in yellow light. See yourself doing what you need to do.

Feel the excitement of taking action. Let your enthusiasm fill your body.

Let yellow fire pour through your eyes, as you allow yourself to see clearly the next step you need to take.

Let it come to you.

Now is the time to act.

Affirmation

- I do what I need to do with enthusiasm, purpose and compassion.

- I Create with vibrant energy all that I desire.

- I trust myself to create what's best for me.

Body Parts - Digestive System, Eyes, Thighs.

Appreciation

See yourself
already having
the changes
you would like.

Give thanks.

Workbook

In what areas of your life could you be more fiery?
Passionate? Enthusiastic?

Are there areas in your life where you feel passive?

Workbook

Now write down those areas on your life where you need
to take action NOW.

My affirmations

Workbook

Pesonal Reflections.

Orange

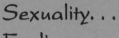

Creativity. . .
Sexuality. . .
Feelings. . .

Orange is the Color of the Water Element

Orange symbolizes our deep reservoir of creativity and intuition, our ability to make connections and flow with our feelings; it is our ability to have and maintain relationships. Orange governs our sensuality and sexuality. Like a dancer, it is our ability to be graceful and fluid, to flow and be creative in every area of our life.

Color Visualization

N ow I'd like you to find a comfortable place that you can relax in. Take a deep breath in. Yes, that's good and now let it out slowly, allowing your thoughts of the day to drift by like goldfish swimming in a beautiful pond one by one they float by under the lilypads as the sun shines down.

You look up and find you are surrounded by tall majestic pine trees and far off in the distance you can see a tall mountain. In the middle of the forest you hear the sound of water tumbling down among the rocks and in the light you see the sun reflecting many colors off a beautiful waterfall. . .

As you begin to relax and feel your facial muscles begin to smooth out, allow yourself to take all the time you need, let the sounds around you merge into one sound, let them comfort you like the sound of the waterfall making its way down the rocks, smoothing over the rocks, finding its way among the sticks and the stones.

Sliding down stone by stone you too can go back to a time when you remember your own very first sensual awakening on a hot summer night perhaps by an old stream.

In the deep stirring of the water you too can recall your own sensuality, and remember now, as you watch the goldfish swim so easily and effortlessly, that first kiss on a warm summer evening, shivering in the moonlit night, how it aroused such tender feelings in you; you can remember just how good you can feel, allowing all those sweet sensations to flow through your body, as you slide gracefully and effortlessly through all those feelings wearing a long robe of orange colors, peach, salmon, flesh tones surrounding your body and making you feel comfortable and alive as you move with ease toward your lover, as easily as sinking in a hot bath, filled with sweet smelling herbs on a cold winter day.

Breathe deeply. See yourself wearing orange tones. Feel the orange sink into your skin. Surround yourself with orange light.

See yourself being more creative, more intuitive.

Feel what its like to be deeply in touch with that essential sensual part of yourself. And as you breathe in the Color Orange, let your feelings come forward, making new connections for yourself.

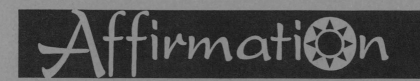

- I trust myself to flow with all the wondrous possibilities of life.

- I am a deeply sensual being.

- I am fluid, graceful and creative.

- I am able to feel all of my feelings.

Body Parts - Feet, Reproductive Organs, Breast

Appreciati☀n

See yourself exactly the way you'd like to be.

Give thanks.

Workbook

Write down those parts of your life where you would like to be more creative, more intuitive, more sensual, be able to flow more, be more graceful.

Are your relationships the way you want them to be?

Are you able to flow with things? How do you deal with
obstacles in your life?

How is your sex drive?

My favorite feeling.

Least favorite feeling.

Workbook

Personal Reflections.

Red

Earth setting limits...
Confidence...
Security...
Stimulation...
Vibrancy...
Structure...

The Color Red is the Element Earth.

It is stimulating, vibrant, magnetic, attracting. Deep shades of red swirl into a majestic red rose and shades of pink. It has tremendous healing potential. Red is strong, vibrant, passionate, exuberant. It draws out, as a poultice does, those qualities we may have deep inside that need to come forward.

Red is the earth and brings in those qualities of the earth - our ability to structure the endless possibilities. It brings in the qualities of feeling secure, feeling safe and nurtured, of Mother Earth.

Earth is the element of our senses, our touch, smell, sight and hearing. Earth is our ability to feel the physical sensations in our bodies. Earth takes its time, is slow and easy like the cows grazing on a hillside on a beautiful sunny day, like the donkey moving down the road at its slow pace, like the turtle safe and protected in its shell. Earth has an enduring patient quality.

Red in all its shades manifests these qualities. It has the ability to draw out our inner lives into an exuberant vitality, allowing us to feel secure, safe, protected and passionate. Taking our time, like the camel; rooted with a strong foundation, unshakable, and persevering...

Color Visualization

Now sit back in your comfortable chair. Bring some cushions in to comfort you. Let your body sink into the softness as your breath rises and falls and your thoughts drift into the color red. Let the sounds around you melt into each other, allowing them to become a part of your experience. Take all the time you need. Even let the small of your neck and back relax.

Now I want you to imagine a bright red ruby shining in the sunlight as you stand on the red-baked earth on a hot summer's day. See yourself as a small girl or boy of 8 or 10, in a puddle of mud. You are trying to uncover a ruby and as you feel the soft wet mud between your fingers you are filled with excitement, you are discovering something. Now return to a time when you had no cares, when there was no real sense of time, only the moment of you and the feeling of the earth turning into small clumps in your hand.

As you breathe in the sweet smell of the red clay, you look out across a field of purple flowers and see a red cardinal spread its wing. Uncovering the ruby, you hold it in your hand, lifting it up to sun as the red winged bird gently swoops down and takes it from your hand, carries it off over the treetops, following a golden ray of sun. . . .

Conscious Daily Exercise

You stand now as an adult, your feet planted in the earth, with that same confidence you had as a child playing in the mud.

Now let those situations, where you need to feel more secure, come into your mind.

Tune in to your breathing.

Color the whole scene Red. See yourself standing in the scene more carefree, more confident. See yourself wearing Red, a red that you love.

Allow the color Red to soak into your body, your feet, securely planted in the earth.

Breathe in red.

Slowly.

Take all the time you need.

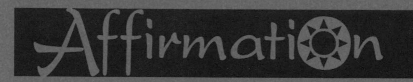

Affirmation

Choose the affirmation most appropriate for you.

• I choose what's best for me

• I focus clearly and do what I need to do.

• I have all the time I need.

• I am a Strong Vibrant Charismatic person and I'm getting more so every day.

Body Parts - Neck, Knees, Colon

Appreciation

See yourself
exactly the way
you'd like to be.

Give thanks.

Are you stimulated by your work. . .by your relationships?
Are there areas in your life where you'd like to feel more confident?

Now list any situations in your life which come to mind where
you need to be more focused, structured.
Where you need to slow down and set limits. . .

Workbook

Do you feel safe and secure?

Are you possessive? Who do I need to let go of?
Do I hold on to people and possessions?

My affirmation.

Workbook

Personal Reflections

Pink

Innocence. . .
Love. . .
Childlike. . .
Softness. . .

Pink is the Color of Love

It is soft, childlike innocence and love. Pink offers the lure of comfort and protection in the world, just like a pink baby blanket envelops a tiny child. Pink is idyllic, like the cherubs, symbolizing the perfection of life and the height of passionate romance.

Color Visualization

Now I want you to sit back and imagine yourself drifting on a raft in a very gentle stream. Let your body relax now, as you breathe in and breathe out, let your facial muscles begin to relax. We are going to take a wonderful journey into pink.

Let your thoughts go by one by one, as the petals of a beautiful pink flower blow off one by one in a gentle breeze. Allow yourself now to be surrounded by pink, a pink light surrounds you everywhere.

Take in a deep breath of pink, and let the rose-colored liquid spill through your body, bringing lightness and softness to your stomach, to your eyes, and the back of your neck as you relax even more deeply.

I want you to imagine yourself in a pink forest surrounded by the most wondrous pink flowers everywhere, each one more brilliant in color than the next, and there in the center of the forest is a circle of pink roses growing so perfectly. As you breathe in the sweet smell of the roses, you can feel your heart opening and warming and softening, as you touch the soft pink petals you bring them to your lips, you can even taste their softness.

See yourself dressed in pink, your favorite pink; feel the healing power of pink, let it warm you, you are safe (red) and feel your innocence (white), like a prince or princess you claim your innocence and confidently step into the center of the circle...

Conscious Daily Exercise

Pink Love Flash

Imagine a situation where you would like to experience more love. Become aware of your breathing.

Imagine the color Rose Pink shining down on you and your loved one in swirling rays of rose pink sweeping over and circling the two of you.

Starting from the bottom of your feet, let the rose pink light wrap around both of you, first around your legs and then up to your hearts and eyes and up to the tops of your heads.

As the pink light rises up to the sun, it meets a green mist, showering down on you from above, filled with golden crystals.

Affirmation

- We are loving each other more and more every day.

- We have a harmonious, deeply fulfilling, passionate relationship and it gets better every day.

- Youth, health, beauty, and strength are mine and I feel better every day.

Body Parts - whole Body, especially Wrinkles

Appreciation

*See and feel
yourself having
what you want.
Affirm now that
what you want
already is.*

Give thanks.

Workbook

Is there an area of your life, that you would like have more fun?
Be more childlike?

Who would you like more love and harmony with right now?

Do you feel nurtured and protected?

How about your relationships, would you like more love? More gentleness, kindness, softness? Respect?

Workbook

Personal Reflections.

Black

Protection. . .
Mystery. . .
Absorbing. . .

Black

Black, the opposite of white, also has the quality of protecting. Black absorbs sun, light and energy. In hot climates it is customary to wear white so as to reflect, not absorb, the heat.

Black is the color of mystery, seduction. It also symbolizes authority. It is the color of sophistication and illusion. Many women wear black because they look thinner. Black is alluring and, at the same time, concealing.

Color Visualization

Black Beauty, a Dark Knight in Shining Armour

It is time now to get comfortable and let your body relax as you take a safe journey into black. Let your mind relax, your arms and toes relax. Now see the color black, its emptiness and its darkness.

Off in the distance you see a large black horse with its shining coat and mane gleaming in the sunlight, wet with sweat; you watch as he gallops off in the distance up the steep mountainside in the dark mist of the evening. You see a man covered from head to toe in black, his cape blowing in the wind as the horse carries him shrouded in mystery, the wind blowing against them.

A dark knight in shining armour disappearing into the darkness... you are safe. . . he will protect you.

Conscious Daily Exercise

Become aware of your breathing.

Feel the darkness surround you in a safe way.

Feel the excitement, the mystery of life hidden in darkness.

When you feel you are too exposed, too bright and you need to tone yourself down (for example on a New York subway), allow a soft protective darkness to surround you.

Affirmation

- I am safe.

- It is safe to be me.

Body Parts -whole Body

Appreciation

See yourself having the qualities you desire.

Give thanks...

Workbook

Describe yourself - are you secretive?
Do you cover things up, protect yourself?

What is your deepest , darkest secret?

Do you absorb other people opinions?

Workbook

Do you have a tendency to hold things in, mull over them, think deeply about something before taking action?

How can I protect myself from too much exposure?

Workbook

Personal Reflections.

White

Magnetic. . .
Purity. . .
Light. . .
Reflecting. . .

White

White is the color of purity and lightness. It is magnetic. When a person walks into a room dressed all in white, attention is immediately drawn to that person.

White symbolizes clarity, and is uplifting. It is often used for protection, it is especially good for people who have trouble setting limits for themselves.

White reflects, it does not absorb.

Color Visualization

Now sit back and get comfortable. Let your body sink into the cushions. Feel the support of the chair beneath you. Feel your breath going in and going out just like waves rise and fall in the ocean.

Now imagine a white light covering everything. Imagine yourself dressed in white, glowing like an angel a luminous white shimmering around you. You peer down into the eyes of a new-born child and see its innocence and you feel yourself pure, clean and fresh as a child.

When you move in white across the open meadow filled with flowers, everyone can see you, they are drawn to you, struck by your innocence and child-like beauty, even the little animals come to sit by your side.

Conscious Daily Exercise

If you find you are in a fearful situation, or have fear of outside influences, consciously surround yourself with white light.

Make sure you call on your fiery yellow power and act if you need to.

- I am clear.

- I am pure.

- I am protected.

Body Parts - whole Body

Appreciation

*See yourself
having the qualities
you desire.*

Give thanks...

Do I hide when I need to let myself become more visible?
In what situations would I like to have more attention?

In what situations could I consciously use more white light to
reflect other peoples effect on me, back to them?

Workbook

Where do I take myself too seriously?
Where do I need to lighten up?

Am I attractive? When I walk into a room do I command attention?

Workbook

Personal Reflections.

Gold

Union. . .
Healing. . .
Sun. . .
Sacred. . .

The Great Healer

Gold is a sacred color and has been found to be wonderful for all kind of physical ailments. When in doubt choose gold.

We find gold in many of the ancient temples. A wedding band is a sacred object, a circle of gold, joining two people.

Color Visualization

The Golden Ring of light

Sit comfortably in your favorite chair and let the thoughts of the week rise up on a ray of light to the sun. Let them burn and dissolve into a single thread of gold light reaching up into the night sky.

As you take a deep breath in, you walk softly through two large golden doors of a very old cathedral; you fall silent as your eyes search the room, in awe of the majestic shining gold columns of light reflecting on to your body. You can feel the luminous gold light reaching into your very cells, healing those places deep inside that need your attention. As the sun touches you through the windows, you can hear the beautiful high pitched tones of children's voices, chanting in the distance. In the golden room of light, you see one small child coming toward you covered in a golden cloth.

The child carries something shining on a soft velvet pillow and offers it to you - a single golden ring of union and healing. And when you take this ring and put it on your finger, everything dissolves back in the light. . .

Conscious Daily Exercise

Take a deep breath in. Imagine a gold light radiating like the sun, like the spokes of a wheel, spinning its rays with each breath, healing and rejuvenating deep into your cellular structure.

As you breathe out, let the breath carry the gold light to all your vital organs, especially the ones that need your attention.

Let your breath fill every part of your body (or someone else's) that needs healing.

Be open to any other colors you'd like to add now.

Swirl this beautiful golden light up your body from your feet all the way to the top of your head and then let it spin off and up to the heavens, returning to the sun.

- I am filled with vibrant health and happiness.

- I feel better and better every day.

- I am capable of healing all parts of my mind, body and soul.

Body Parts - whole Body

Appreciation

See yourself whole, healthy and happy.

Give thanks.

Workbook

What part of your body needs attention or healing at this time?

Who do you know that would like to send a gold
healing light?

Workbook

Is there an area in your life that needs to be kept more sacred?

Workbook

Personal Reflections.

Violet

Wisdom. . .
Guidance. . .
Spirituality. . .
Self-trust. . .
Transcendence. . .

Violet is the Color of Spiritual Enlightenment

Violet, in all its wonderful shades of lavender and purple symbolizes our inner knowing, our wisdom, getting in touch with the spiritual part of ourselves that truly knows what is best for us, the part of ourselves beyond our problems of everyday life.

Violet is a spiritual color, symbolizing truth, transcendence and guidance. It is the color that guides us to a higher source of knowledge and spiritual enlightenment. Poetry, music and art flourish under the color of violet.

Color Visualization

Now get comfortable and allow your body to find a relaxing position, one where you don't have to do anything, let your thoughts go now as you breathe in gently and easily and breathe out allowing all your muscles to relax even deeper.

And now imagine the color violet, beautiful deep rich hues of violet. Imagine yourself clothed in long purple robes, like a great king or queen on an ancient throne long ago. As you let your thoughts drift away like leaves blowing across a field on a warm day, let everything around you, melt into the color purple.

Imagine purple streams of water filling your body; as you breathe in, feel it fill your lungs, your heart, even your eyes, and as you exhale, see yourself standing among a field of violet flowers in a very far away time, as you allow your muscles to relax even more deeply, you can feel the purple liquid run through your body dissolving all the tense places.

Bathe yourself in violet light as you walk slowly, in your purple robes of royalty, with ease and grace across a field of purple flowers. You come to a very old stream and sit down on the green grass. You look down and gaze into a purple pool of water and as the sun shines from above, you can see your reflection. As you look closer, you can see stirring in the violet waters another reflection; you look into the eyes of a very old woman.

She has the most compassionate and wise eyes, her long white hair swirls in the water and from her wrinkled face she peers at you with violet eyes, all-knowing and wise. . . and so you ask her many things and listen closely as she answers each and every one of them.

Conscious Daily Exercise

Breathe.

Violet surrounds you.

Let your questions be surrounded in a violet light.

See yourself trusting yourself to know the answers, contacting your inner wisdom.

Give thanks...

Affirmation

- I have the wisdom to know what's best for me.

- I have the courage to act on what I know is best for me.

- I trust myself.

Body Parts - Crown, Top of Head

Appreciation

See yourself
exactly the way you
would like to be.

Give Thanks. . .

Workbook

Write down the situations in your life which may confuse you,
where there doesn't seem to be any resolution, color them in violet.

Do you trust other people?

Who don't you trust?

Workbook

When? Why?

Do you trust yourself?

What is your favorite type of music?
How does it make you feel?

Workbook

Personal Reflections.

Color Trance-Formation

Color Reality

See yourself exactly as you are in your present life situation.
Don't exaggerate. Be honest. Write it down.

What are your favorite colors?

Color Trance-Formation

Color Vision

How would you like your life to be? No holds barred. Nothing
is too far-fetched. Write out your true visions, your dreams.
Don't think about all the reasons why it can't work.

What colors come to you now?

Now take the colors you have come up with and spin
them together. Write down your experiences.

New Dimensions in Sound and Color

Sounds create vibrations. When we tap two tuning forks together the sound created is called an interval. The vibrations of different intervals correspond to the vibrations of different colors.

Due to the revolutionary work of John Beaulieu we now have available to us tuning forks that vibrate to the different frequencies of the colors and their corresponding elements.

When we listen to the sound of an interval, our body attempts to resolve the differences between the two tones. Our nervous system naturally tunes to the vibrations of the color or element, and we become more relaxed.

Tuning forks can deepen your experience of color by adding sound. Tapping them after your Visualization and Conscious Daily Exercises brings the healing vibration of your color even deeper into your cellular structure.

See enclosed order form to order "Music and Sound in the Healing Arts" and Tuning Forks for the Colors and Elements.

Color Splash Dance

Overall Color Cleansing

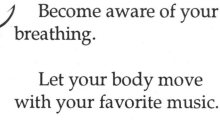

Become aware of your breathing.

Let your body move with your favorite music.

Let the colors swirl up your body crossing in a figure eight motion in rainbow colors from right to left and then left to right.

Start at the feet and breathe and swirl orange, red, yellow, green, blue, pink, and violet in figure 8's, white, gold, black dissolving into white and then spinning off the top of your head like a star shooting across the sky.

Then shower yourself, standing as still as possible, with your favorite color.

Order form

Feel free to give the Gift of Color to your friends. Now that you've discovered how much fun you can have with the **"Color Love Journal"** why not share it with a friend. You can order extra copies by filling out and mailing the easy order form below.

Save $2.00 or more by ordering more than one copy.

POLARITY WELLNESS CENTER INC.
RAINBOW HARMONICS DIVISION
10 Leonard St. #2A, New York, NY 10013
YES, send me more copies of the **"Color Love Journal"**!

Send one copy for **$9.95***	
SAVE $1.00 on each book by ordering two or more copies:	
Send _____ copies at **$8.95** each	
Postage/Handling: **$1.50** first book **+50¢ each** additional*	
NYS residents add 8.25% Sales Tax	
PAYMENT ENCLOSED (Check or money order)	

Print Name_____

Address_____

City_____State_____Zip_____

*1992 prices subject to change.

POLARITY WELLNESS CENTER INC.
RAINBOW HARMONICS DIVISION
10 Leonard St. #2A, New York, NY 10013
YES, send me more copies of the "Color Love Journal"!

Send one copy for **$9.95***	
SAVE $1.00 on each book by ordering two or more copies:	
Send _____ copies at **$8.95** each	
Postage/Handling: **$1.50** first book **+50¢** each additional*	
NYS residents add 8.25% Sales Tax	
PAYMENT ENCLOSED (Check or money order)	

Print Name_____

Address_____

City_____State_____Zip_____
*1992 prices subject to change.

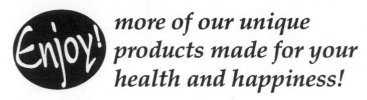
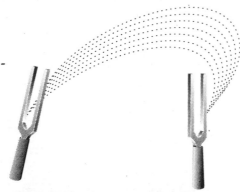

POLARITY WELLNESS CENTER INC.
RAINBOW HARMONICS DIVISION
10 Leonard St. #2A, New York, NY 10013

RAINBOW HARMONY Set *with Recycled Carring Bag* - **$30.00**	
MUSIC AND SOUND IN THE HEALING ARTS - **$11.95**	
RAINBOW MEDITATIONS, *Audio Cassette* - **$15.00**	
Postage/Handling: **$3.50**	
NYS residents add 8.25% Sales Tax	
TOTAL	
PAYMENT INCLOSED (Check or money order)	

YES, I would like to be on your mailing list.

Print Name_____

Address_____

City_____State_____Zip_____

POLARITY WELLNESS CENTER INC.
RAINBOW HARMONICS DIVISION
10 Leonard St. #2A, New York, NY 10013

RAINBOW HARMONY Set *with Recycled Carring Bag* - **$30.00**	
MUSIC AND SOUND IN THE HEALING ARTS - **$11.95**	
RAINBOW MEDITATIONS, *Audio Cassette* - **$15.00**	
Postage/Handling: **$3.50**	
NYS residents add 8.25% Sales Tax	
TOTAL	
PAYMENT INCLOSED (Check or money order)	

YES, I would like to be on your mailing list.

Print Name_____

Address_____

City_____State_____Zip_____

For information on classes, workshops, please write to us.
We welcome your comments and experienes.

POLARITY WELLNESS CENTER INC.
RAINBOW HARMONICS DIVISION
10 Leonard St. #2A, New York, NY 10013